CONTENTS

RISING
FROM THE
ASHES

E. JEAN JOHNSON

ACKNOWLEDGEMENTS

To my children, who loved me through it all, even when you didn't understand it. Thank you for covering me through prayers, words of affirmation, encouragement and support, but especially your love!

None of these words that I could ever put pen to paper will ever express the depth of my love for each of you. You are the hope that God gave me to survive it all. I love you more than you'll ever know!

My Fav 5!
VERNON, VANCE, CHANDRA,
EARL and JOSHUA

SPECIAL ACKNOWLEDGMENT

To MIKE, you told me in the beginning of our marriage that you had big shoes to fill. Thank you for filling your own shoes and walking the path that God set for you. Thank you for growing and maturing to the man that you have become. Thank you for the love and support that you have always embraced us with. Thank you for always providing for us immeasurably! Thank you for 21 years thus far, when the world was against us! Thank you for loving me and patiently waiting for my love to grow for you. I love you!

Now let's turn the page to see what God has in store for us in our next chapter as our journey continues....

IN LOVING MEMORY....

Earline Johnson Jackson (mama)

James Nicholas Jr. (daddy)

Lorna Nannette Allen (sister)

Herkisha Lashay Young (niece)

Earl L. Coleman Jr. (friend)

DEDICATION

This book is dedicated to the loving memory of EARL JAMES LITTLE JR.

The messenger of the Lord that stood in the gap for me when I was lost in sin and couldn't find my way. You introduced me to Jesus and loved me to salvation in Christ Jesus.

To the husband that showed me what real love was, the man that loved me, honored, respected and cared for me when I didn't know how to love myself.

To the man that stole my heart through his kindness, generosity, integrity and strength. A man of faith, prayer, and Godliness. A wonderful provider and protector.

To the father who didn't see another man's children but saw an extension of me and embraced them as his own, through his love for them.

Somehow, I think that you always knew who I was and why I was in your life. This story would not be possible without you. I also think that I was your assignment from God because God knew that you would give me and my children the love we needed.

I am the woman I am because of you being the example of Godliness, faithfulness and truth.

Thank you for loving me through all of my flaws, weaknesses and failures. Thank you for being the example of Jesus in our home.

Thank you for leaving the greatest part of you behind - your seed - who walk in the same integrity of their father, our sons, Earl III and Joshua.

You are forever in my heart. I miss you, man of God - love always.

FOREWORD

When we met in Denham Springs, Louisiana many years ago, neither of us had any idea what God was doing. Our relationship is a demonstration of faith, hope, grace and love. In fact, we met at Greater Faith Outreach Ministries, a church where everyone felt like family. I still love and adore Pastors Joe and Katheran Mitchell, their children and the members. This is where I met Jean and her family. It was always a pleasant experience.

Fast forward a few years and a few major life changes, Jean and her family moved to Maryland. We reconnected and became very close. Jean and her beautiful family seemed to always have a glow of hope. It's one of the things I've admired about her. She was always smiling regardless of what was going on in her life. She never looked like what she had been through or what she was going through. She was then and still is today the embodiment of grace.

In order to rise from the ashes, the way she has, one must be committed to keep showing up for love. No matter what life brings your way keep showing up. As you read her words you will see this pattern. All her life, regardless of how many lemons life brought into her life, Jean managed to make sweet lemonade. As you journey through her riveting story of trouble, tragedy, trauma and triumph, you too will come to admire the way Jean keeps showing up for love.

The only way anyone can rise from the ashes is to come through fire. God has certainly given Jean beauty for ashes. As you read this book you will laugh, cry, get angry, be shocked and ultimately be inspired to do what Jean has done. Keep showing up for love. Keep energizing your faith. Keep your hope alive. Know that the purpose of every fire moment in your life is to cause you to rise from the ashes with a deep understanding that God's grace is indeed amazing.

The best is yet to come!

Dr. Vikki Johnson
Chaplain, Speaker, Author & Creator, Soul Wealth
www.vikkijohnson.com

ASHES

1. Something that symbolizes grief, repentance, or humiliation

2. Residue left from materials thoroughly burned

3. A dark, unproductive place mentally or emotionally

Merriam Webster Dictionary

CHAPTER 1

WHERE DO I START?

What about the domestic violence, the abuse, the illnesses, multiple marriages and adulteries endured in some of them? The anger, frustrations and secrets. The thoughts and feelings of not being good enough - .insecurities - the death of my husband and murder of my sister?

In life, we will experience tragedies and triumphs, victories and defeats, break ups and hook ups, marriage and divorce, life and death. But in all of this, know that there exists a healthy place for us.

A healthy place resides in you, in your mind and emotions. It's a place where your mind can rest, and you can be assured that all of your questions will be answered.

A place where there's no frustrations, anger or numbness. You may be asking yourself "why am I experiencing life's trials and tribulations like this?"

Am I crazy, or what's really going on?

No, you're not crazy, you're just tired of dealing with crazy and you want a way out!

It's possible to be free, safe and in that healthy place, mind, soul and spirit, and I'll tell you how I overcame.

For years, I had been in a cave, a place of discouragement, frustration, depression, confusion and turmoil. I lost all hope, I needed help and peace. I totally believe in God, His word, and his son, Jesus Christ, but I couldn't pray, or read the bible. I didn't even have the desire to go to church most of the time.

I just felt numb, existing but not living, enduring but unhappy, and I allowed bitterness and anger to eat away my healthy place. I didn't have peace of mind and I had trust issues. I couldn't trust, due to the pain of betrayal in some of my marriages…yes marriages-- 4 of them to be exact.

Was I living a lie? Covering up my truths with smiles and makeup? Looking like happiness on the outside but dying on the inside?

No, we don't need to air all of our dirty laundry, but we don't need to pretend either. I have never been good at pretending, I'm a straight shooter and I have to be honest, at least with myself.

We need to ask ourselves:

> Am I happy?
>
> Is it worth this?
>
> Is this the reality of my life?
>
> Can this be salvaged?
>
> Is this too good to leave, but too bad to stay?

On a merry go round, going around and around the mountain but never going UP… never getting to a new place or higher heights…never reaching the top! Fighting the same ole demons that have held you bound for years and never breaking free to live an unchained life.

When is enough truly enough?

Where is change?

Why the vicious cycle?

How do I break free?

When does the madness stop?

Can any good thing come out of
the ashes?

I was tired of being in dark places of depression, living an unproductive life, living sound one moment and grief stricken the next, joyful here, sad there, heavenly happiness today and fire and brimstone hell tomorrow. I felt humiliated and ashamed of the residue of my past for things that I didn't do, while trying to protect and cover up somebody else's mess! I felt like a sign was on my forehead that read "FAILURE"!

Deep down inside, you know that you are not a failure, but you have been made to FEEL like a failure by someone else. Why do we measure ourselves by someone else's measuring stick, when you know you're awesome all by yourself? It's all mind games, tricks, manipulation and deception. I felt like I was being targeted and hunted like a wild animal only to be captured for the slaughter. That's how it feels when you're played with or used for sport.

We don't connect with someone for game, we connect because our emotional heart strings pull us in your direction and says, "I like you too." I was tired of trying to figure you out when I couldn't figure me out. I shouldn't have to figure you out like a math problem when we both should be each other's solution in a relationship.

We have analyzed ourselves, changed our hair, our bodies, our walk and everything we could think of to make ourselves better, when we did not realize that we were already our best! It's time to stop the madness! We have to be our authentic selves and stop creating "Barbie" to fit a superficial relationship. It's too much work and it's not worth it. Why should we dress up a lie, or paint a picture of perfection when it's not real? We feel so much better when we can just be ourselves. Ask yourself, "Who am I?" If you can't answer that question, you've lost yourself. You have become who someone else made you to be based on the role they have given you and not who you know that you are.

What role are you playing?

Are you a cartoon character, who is not taken seriously in the relationship, to amuse and be laughed at?

Are you a porn star, in a relationship just for someone else's pleasure, to take them to the moon and back and not hear from them again until they are ready for their next trip?

Are you playing an action role, constantly running for your life, and jumping through hoops of abuse, playing hide and seek, ducking punches and trying to plan your next move when you can't get out?

Or are you the object of someone's affection in a romance novel. Someone that wants to look into your eyes, with a pounding heart of excitement that says, "I love you". Someone whose world you change just by your mere presence. Someone that couldn't imagine life without you and makes you feel special, like the queen you are.

Think about it and you decide. It's all up to you. You know who you are, you know how you want to feel. It's time to flip the script and be the wonderful, amazing, lovely woman that you know you are full of happiness and peace!

It took me years, but I found myself.

CHAPTER 2

IN THE BEGINNING

I grew up in a small town in Louisiana where we only had one red light. My life was simple, and my playground was the sugarcane fields. I loved growing up with standards of southern hospitality, the bond and closeness of community that surrounded me, and the feeling of everyone being or becoming family.

Everyone knew everyone. Giving and sharing with each other was a part of our daily lifestyle. We lived in what we call a shotgun house, you walk in the front door and straight out of the back door through every room in the house.

My family consisted of my mother, stepfather, two sisters and myself. My stepfather was a wonderful man that took care of my mother and us. He was a police officer and school bus driver. My mother was a very, hard working woman, even though my stepfather never wanted her to work, she always believed that a woman should have her own. Mama was beautiful and kind but strong. I admired her strengths as well as her disciplines, but her expectations of me as the eldest were sometimes overwhelming. My two sisters were younger and very pretty with long hair and lighter skin, we were always compared by people that would address me as the black one, which made me feel like that was a bad thing. Mama was very strict, especially on me as the oldest and I hated that, but as I look back now, I'm very grateful for the way I was raised because there were standards, manners and respect for our elders as well as each other.

I thought that the role that I was given was a little unfair because most of the responsibilities fell on me. I didn't mind chores, but I didn't like the amount that was thrust upon me. I had to be the example. I loved my sisters, but I wasn't excited about being second mom, which included cooking, cleaning, laundry, washing and combing their hair, giving them their baths, and putting them to bed.

One thing was sure, I was groomed to be a wife and mother. Mama was also a seamstress, baker and cook, so I learned to lay and cut out patterns for her to make dresses or whatever she was sewing. I remember being in the kitchen around age 9 and making dresses by 13.

Our home always smelled like a bakery, with fresh baked pastries or pecan candy cooking on the stove because mama cooked for the neighborhood as well as baked or sewed for whomever needed or wanted it. I dreamed of the day when I would just be able to live my own life.

I have always been a dreamer. I would dream things in my sleep that would come to reality, so my mom never wanted me to share any bad dream with her, and I would daydream about things I hoped would come into my future, but being a housewife and doing what mama did, was never a part of my dreams. I wanted to be an actress!

My dream world was where I lived in my free time. I would even stand in front of the mirror pretending to be an actress, living in Hollywood and seeing myself on the big screen. I remember telling mama that one day I would be rich, and she responded by saying that there's nothing wrong with dreaming, just make sure that you wake up to the real world! Mama was no nonsense and a jack of all trades and that part of her, I desired more than anything. I loved being around her because I loved her creativity and her strength.

I always enjoyed being with family, in my younger days, my great-Aunt Mary would babysit us. She was amazing! She was small in stature but a giant in my eyes that could do anything! I would watch her lift heavy things, work in her yard, take care of the chickens, pump water, build and repair things, and that was very attractive to me because she was so independent! Five of my cousins lived there, all girls, Debra, Sarah, Dianne, Willie Mae, and Lois and I loved to be there with them. She would play with us and wrestle with us, but she was a strict disciplinarian; she didn't play when times of having to be disciplined were presented! I learned so much from her because she was a very strong and wise woman and everyone that knew her, respected her. She was more of a grandmother to me, instead of an aunt because she raised my mother and my aunt Mercedes, after the loss of their parents.

You could easily tell that my mom had been around Aunt Mary, because a lot of Aunt Mary was in my mom, especially when it came to work ethics, order and strict discipline. As a teenager, I began to rebel, because I just wanted to be a teenager and not have the "mama" responsibilities of taking care of children. I do understand that as an older child, you should help your younger siblings, but where was my childhood, and at this point, where was my teen life? I never remember playing with dolls or games or doing what kids do, and in my teen years, I'm still the "Mother hen" and it wasn't fair to me.

I also no longer felt the need of community discipline, you know, where even the neighbor could tag your behind! I was old enough to do everything else but I still wasn't allowed to go certain places or get involved in certain activities that other teenagers would normally do because I wasn't free until mama got home from work and even after she got home, I had more things to do. I remember making the track team at school, coming home all excited, and mama telling me that I couldn't participate because I had to take care of my sisters, but one thing she would let me do when all of my chores was done, was go to some of my friend's houses.

I lived on the same street as one of my friends, her name was Sandra, and mama allowed me to go to her house sometimes. She lived with her grandparents and a cousin. Her cousin was a guy that I knew from school but never really had any conversations. He was a grade higher than I was and handsome, very muscular, an athlete of course. He had a beautiful smile that would make you melt, you know, that beautiful Michael Jackson smile. He was popular and extremely smart and awesome in any sport that he played. We called him Rocky.

Everybody wanted a piece of the "Rock". Teachers wanted him in their classes because he was extremely smart and a straight A student in every subject. Nothing was a challenge for him. Coaches wanted him because he excelled in every sport he played and was great at basically everything. Of course, the girls wanted him for all of the above and more. Everyone wanted to be around him just because of who he was. I later found out that his mom went to college at a very young age, so I guess that's where he gets his genius.

Every time I hung out with Sandra, he would tease me or say something mean to me, so I thought that he didn't like me, only to find out that he did. After a while we started talking more and we really enjoyed being around each other. It blew my mind how smart he truly was! One day, he came over and asked my mom if he could court me…(yeah, that was way back in the day). She interviewed him like she was considering hiring him for a job! She gave him her conditions and finally said yes. I was praying hard that she would say yes. We couldn't stay away from each other, every ounce of free time we had was with each other. We had to see each other every day! I made sure that all of my work was done and that all of my sisters needs were met so that nothing would interfere with our time together….yep, young love. He would make me do my homework and help me with it. I remember one day I had to take a math test and I really struggled in math, he came to the window of the building where I sat, with pencil and paper and took the test for me, without the teacher knowing that he was right outside of the window. I copied everything he wrote and passed the test! I still can't believe that we got away with that! Life with Rocky was sweet…I fell so hard for him that at times, I think I loved him more than I loved myself. I know that this sounds crazy but remember, we were just kids in high school. We were just teenagers then and we started doing what some teenagers do, and that lead to something that we weren't ready for. Mama found out that we started having sex and blew a fuse! She asked us if we were ready for marriage and informed us that she would be talking to his mother soon about marriage. We told her that we didn't want to get married and she then forbade him to see me anymore; shortly after, I found out that I was pregnant.

16 years old and pregnant! About to have a real baby! Rocky's baby, and that made me very happy, knowing that a part of him was growing inside of me. I was a lovesick puppy and mama was on level 100! I remember the day that she went to his family's home with the news, it was one of the scariest days of my life!

I knew his mom and she was a wonderful woman that I admired, but Rocky was her only child, and I expected her to be upset. She had high hopes for her son and that didn't include him being a father at 17! But she was also intelligent, levelheaded, and straight forward and definitely didn't bite her tongue. She needed answers and time to digest this news as she tried to figure out the best solution for everyone, but marriage was the only thing on mama's mind!

We truly loved each other, but marriage was not on our minds either. Of course, we wanted our baby, but we also wanted graduation and college and a future. We felt that marriage at this age would alter our futures. Our plans for college were shattered and Rocky enlisted in the marine corps so that he would be able to support his new family. I loved the idea because of the military lifestyle, the order, discipline and accountability. I believed that this would shape him into the man, husband and father that he was to become.

I stayed home while he left for boot camp waiting to have the baby; 16 years old, waiting to have a baby. I had to drop out of high school because you couldn't go to school pregnant back in those days and you were frowned on because of the fact that you were indeed pregnant as a teenager. All of my friends were banned by their parents to stay away from me, I guess I was a bad influence because I was pregnant. I was starred at like I was something that was never seen before, laughed at because of my growing belly, and talked about as though I had committed a crime. I was so hurt and ashamed of being made to feel like I was nothing and that I ruined someone else's life. I didn't do this by myself! I was so blinded by love; I didn't see any of this coming.

I thought more about Rocky's life than I did my own, because he was a brilliant mind that could have been anything he wanted to be in life, and I felt like I took that away from him. It was hard to see all of our plans just go up in smoke, but we did what we each thought was right, especially for our baby.

One month after my 17th birthday, I gave birth to baby boy, Vernon Jr. (Rocky's name). He was the spitting image of his father! This changed my whole life and I was so happy to have a part of me and Rocky in this one little, beautiful person, who also turned out to be just as smart as his dad.

We got married, and I went back to high school and graduated. When my baby was about 6 months old, we moved to North Carolina where he was stationed. It was exciting to be a military wife and meet all of the other military families. I was one of the youngest, of the wives in our community, so the other wives really looked out for me and sometimes treated me like I was their teenage daughter. I was very excited about military life because I was accustomed to structure, order and discipline, I was happy there, but I missed my family. I missed mama and Jack (my stepfather), Nay and Baba (Nedra and Lorna) my sisters but I knew that I was a wife and mother now and I had to grow up fast.

I was just a kid playing house, not really knowing what I was doing. I knew how to cook, clean, organize and take care of my baby, but I didn't know how to discern the signs. I didn't know how to read what was going on with my husband. I noticed that he was a little different when I moved there, but I thought that it was just him being military.

After being there for a few months, he began to be mean and impatient with me, and his words were sharp and cold, and everything seemed to bother him. I felt like he didn't really want me there. I thought that I was about to hear him scream at me about how I messed his life up! I tried to talk to him about things, but he didn't want to talk. I tried everything I could to make him happy so that we could fix what was wrong, but nothing worked. So I asked him the question that every woman wants to know, in times like this, is there someone else? I got the shock of my life, expecting him to say no and go on to explain his change, instead he said YES! I couldn't move, I was speechless. Tears began to run down my face, and I felt like someone had just punched me in the gut. I asked him how he could do that to me he said, "I'm just who I am baby". He didn't seem sorry for hurting me. He didn't seem to care and almost sounded cocky and arrogant, so I began to pack me and my baby's things and then it happened. He stood up walked over to me, looked me in the eyes and slapped me to the floor! The shock of it all turned my stomach. I felt sick and confused--he had never hit me before! He had never been so cold! Who was this man and where was the man of my dreams? He said to me, you're not leaving me, and don't you ever try, and you better not tell anybody ... for the first time in my life I became afraid of him. I went in the bathroom and cleaned my bloody nose and I cried, I didn't have anywhere to run, no family, no safe place, I was stuck...so I stayed and kept quiet. I was stunned at the fact that he hit me, and I was afraid to tell anybody, after all he was Rocky-- everybody loved him. I was just the one who messed up his life by getting pregnant. Who would believe me anyway? I knew that I had to get away, because if he hit me because HE was committing adultery, what would happen next?

He started hanging out with the boys more and more and doing what he apparently was doing before I got there. I wanted to call mama but she wouldn't believe me, she never saw that side of him, and I was afraid that he would find out if I did, so my days were filled with tears, sadness and regret, being slapped, kicked or punched became a lifestyle.....my new normal. You never really know a person until you live with them.

As time passed, I became pregnant again but due to the violence, I lost that child the night I told him, and I gained a black eye and a cut lip! I became sport for him, and I realized that a lot of his frustrations was because I was the wrong woman, I was stuck! The violence and adulteries escalated to the point that he no longer tried to hide his women, and I really couldn't believe all of the things that was happening between us. I became so afraid of him that I wouldn't ask certain questions like, how much was the utility bill or even tell him that I needed milk! How could a love so sweet turn into this! a multitude of hurt, fighting, and even being thrown out of the house! I was afraid of the threats; I was afraid to leave but I was also afraid to stay! I constantly lived in fear, especially of telling anyone what was going on, but I wanted to, I needed to. How could such a wonderful person seem to change overnight? I loved him and I thought that we would be together for the rest of our lives, but not this person, not this man that didn't respect me at all!

The love I had for him turned to remorse and all I dreamed of was the day I could get away from him.

His unit had to go in the field for 2 weeks and if ever there was a time to run, that was it! One night after his unit left for the field, my baby and I were asleep and I heard someone breaking into the house, I grabbed the baby, went into the closet and hid behind the clothes, I covered my baby's mouth and stayed there until I heard them leave. I thank God that the baby stayed asleep and I called the Police, I knew it was time for me to leave because I took this incident as a sign that this was my window of freedom! The next day his paycheck came, so I forged it, cashed it and called a cab for the airport. I grabbed only my baby's diaper bag and a change of clothes because I didn't want him to know that I was gone, so I left everything!

After getting home, I never told mama what happened, I just told her that he was in the field and about the break in and that I was scared to stay there alone. After he came out of the field and couldn't find me, he called his mom and she told him that I was there. A few days later, he came to my mom's house at four in the morning and threatened me with a gun. I asked if I could spend the next day with the family and then I would come back, all the while planning to call the Marine Corps office and tell them what happened. When he came to get me the following day, the Marines were waiting to take him back.

I had to run away to save myself, I had to run away to protect my child. I had lost a child, myself and my identity, I no longer knew who I was. I had given the very core of who I was, to a man that didn't understand the purpose of a wife, and when you don't know the purpose of a thing, you will abuse it! I allowed my weaknesses that were fueled by fear, to become his strengths.

CHAPTER 3

OUR CHOICES

I recently heard a Pastor say that "we are born looking like our parents, but we die looking like our choices."

I have made many impulsive choices in my life, and many of the hurts, pains and disappointments that I suffered, were direct results of those choices.

Becoming a wife and mother as a teenager was not a wise choice, but I have to say that becoming a mother gave me a sense of purpose. I had someone to live for, other than myself. I had someone to love and nurture and take care of, someone that would love me for real.

We really shouldn't just make choices on a whim, without weighing all of our options, pondering them in our hearts or better yet, praying about them. We should question ourselves about every decision that we're about to make. However, at that time I was a child. I wasn't strong enough or wise enough! I loved him, but at what cost? We don't realize the magnitude of the power that we possess as women, especially when you're being torn down and constantly abused…We don't know our worth.

I just wanted to breathe, and go on with my life, just wanted to be free to enjoy life and find normal! About a year later, I finally went to college. I commuted by bus everyday about 80 miles back and forth the first semester. Before my second semester started, I asked mama if she would keep my son for that semester because the commute was hard, having to be at the bus stop at 530 am every morning and getting home at 630 pm, she said yes and I moved on campus.

Being away from my son was very hard but I talked to him every day and came home most weekends. My goal was to give him the life I never had, and I had to get a degree to do that.

After moving on campus, I was introduced to a whole new lifestyle that I loved, and I fell in love with Baton Rouge! I had made up my mind that once I finished school that I would be saying bye- bye to my hometown. I loved life on campus! I could finally find me and make my own decisions as to my future. I embraced the books, the studying, the projects and homework and all that came with it. My roommates would take turns going to each other's homes for the weekend and wanted to come to my home town one weekend, I told them that there was nothing to do in my hometown because it was very small and didn't have the attractions of other towns. They suggested just hanging out at the mall, I said we have no mall. They suggested going to a movie, I told them that we have no movie theatres. Then they said that we could just go to a restaurant and have dinner. I said we have no restaurants, and that whatever they wanted to do, we'd have to come back to Baton Rouge to do. They never asked again. I embraced my life at this point and never looked back. I didn't hate Rocky, we were just kids, but I knew that he wasn't the man for me. He was my son's father and I would always respect him as that, but as for me and him, that was clearly over.

One of my cousins lived on campus and told me that his roommate wanted to meet me. Not interested because of the hell I had previously come out of but wanting to be polite, I agreed to meet. He was a musician in the marching band, a tall handsome guy that wanted to get to know me. He had a cute little studder when he spoke and was very charming and easy to talk to, but I was straight up with him and told him my situation. He suggested that we be just friends, after all, we all needed someone to talk to, and we talked every day and began to spend more time together. He was a breath of fresh air, just easy to be around. The more time we spent together the more I started to like him and quickly fell for him. I don't know why I fell so quickly, maybe because he was just something different, or maybe I wasn't getting my face redecorated or maybe I must have just been in the house too long with no social life, I don't know…. Oh, his name was Cliff. I was comfortable with him and for some reason, I trusted him…. I became pregnant again, broken hearted and afraid. I already had my first son, no husband and struggling to build a life for him, and now I found myself pregnant again and afraid to tell him! I felt like I just couldn't get ahead! I didn't know how he would feel, all I knew was that I loved him, and I hoped that he would be happy about our baby! I didn't tell him for a while because I wanted to enjoy the happiness that I felt when I was around him and the thought of all of that falling apart was scary to me. I would cry most of the time because I was emotional due to the pregnancy and I also cried because of the fear I felt of losing him. When the time of revelation came, he walked out of my life and never looked back! I felt like nothing, I felt so used, hurt and angry. I had to drop out of school because of morning sickness and it was also embarrassing throwing up at any given time.

I told my roommates that I was leaving and why, and I found out that another roommate was leaving also because she was pregnant and sickly, and pregnant for Cliff!!!!! I wanted to talk to him because I needed answers, but he wouldn't answer or return any of my calls. It took me that long to realize that he was a player and was no good! When the time of delivery came, I had many complications, hemorrhaging being one of them and I almost lost my life. I discovered that I had twins but one of them didn't survive. The doctor told me that he wasn't fully developed but it was a boy and that tore me to pieces. I had a dead baby, I had two children for a man that didn't care. He had two sons and didn't even know it! I named them Vance and Lance. It was a bittersweet birth because one lived and one died and mama was the only one there to love on me, through all of this.

He had great acting skills because he made me feel so loved and cared for, but his true colors showed when he walked out of my life when I needed him most.

Vance was a beautiful baby. He was very fair with greenish gray eyes and always smiled. He was my happy baby and I loved him. I no longer cared that his father wasn't there - I would love him and take care of him without his father. Vance was mine; Vernon was mine and that's all that mattered.

When Vance was about seven months old, mama asked me to ride to Baton Rouge with her and I brought Vance with me. We went into a store that I didn't know his father worked in and when we walked in, there he was. When I told mama who he was, she walked over to him, told him a few choice words, and she insisted that he look at his son! When he saw me, it was as if he'd seen a ghost. He just froze and didn't say anything. Mama had a whole lot to say but I was just done with him! I assured him that we didn't need or want anything from him, ever! Done with these crazy men and their lies! Done with the pains of these relationships! Just done!

My son turned out to be a musician just like his father, even more awesome because God blessed him to play all kinds of instruments, and we never saw or heard from his father again.

I didn't understand why I kept failing.

What was I doing wrong?

Was something wrong with me or was it just desperation?

Am I just a weak person?

Was this true love or did I love the idea of being in love?

How can you truly love someone one minute and hate them the next?

My mind was flooded with questions that I couldn't answer but one thing gave me peace and that was the fact that this time, I wasn't beaten, bloody, or bruised. It was wonderful, but it was all a lie, and he was a liar and a player, and I got played. That's the reality of that relationship. I couldn't get mad at anyone but myself. He was good at what he did, he had to be, to date roommates and neither of us know! To make 2 babies! How, when we spent so much time together? That was a lesson and I still had more to learn. That was a bad choice, not a mistake, but a choice!

I didn't think about what the outcome could have been, I just wanted someone to love me. I didn't think anything over, I didn't stay focused on school, and again I allowed someone else to have all of the control.

In the midst of all of the hurt and pain of both of these men, I realized that they had given me treasures… two adorable hearts that I could love forever, and that was the good that came out of those ashes!

I dropped out of school to take care of my boys, moved back to mama's house, with plans to finish school after the baby got a little older. One day Rocky came over, he was out of the military by then and he wanted to see his son and congratulate me on the baby. He apologized for the way he treated me and asked for forgiveness and we talked for hours. He shared his relationships and I shared what happened with Cliff. He said that he hoped that we could be friends, and all of this brought closure for me. I still cared about him, but I knew that being his wife was something that I no longer desired.

I thank God that my children were young and didn't know or understand any of this, but I knew that it was time to go in "Mother hen" mode and protect them. Rocky started coming by every day and he would even take me and the boys riding sometimes. His mother came by to see the baby and I assured her that he was not Rocky's child, especially with fair skin and greenish gray eyes. She said something to me that I will never forget. She said as far as she was concerned, he had her last name, so he belonged to her too! That was the sweetest, kindest thing that any mother-in-law could say to you, knowing that Vance was not her biological grandchild, but she loved him just the same. To this day, her family has always loved my son and never treated him any different from his brother.

His mother has always been kind to me, that's why I never wanted her to know the things I endured with her son. She always made sure that I had everything I needed and wanted, even though I was no longer with her son. She had a home that she only lived in on weekends because she lived and worked in another city. She allowed me to move in her house along with the boys so that we'd have our own space. Mama's house had become too crowded.

Things were going great, but Rocky wanted to reconcile. I had accepted his apology, but I was afraid to say no to trying love again with him, especially since I now had another man's child and the fact that fear was still there. He also reminded me that technically it was his house and I couldn't really stop him from moving in, so, I made a fool move and let him back in. It wasn't long before the sleeping around started again. I wasn't going to fight and argue with him again, so I kept quiet and started planning my next move. Again, he begged me not to leave and promised me that he would never do it again, tears and all. He seemed sincere. After all, he forgave me for having another man's child, so how could I not forgive him, right? So, I stayed, and it was all right for a while, then I found out about another affair and that was it! I held my head up and walked out and dared him to say anything to me! I wasn't afraid anymore! The anger that I felt, ran fear off! I had to tell myself not to be his fool anymore; that I don't owe him anything! I had to free myself! I had to stop allowing him in and out of my life at will without true change. Women and drugs would always be his priority over me!

I couldn't understand why I would allow this all over again! You feel like nothing when you're cheated on, or beaten, or constantly lied to, but what I really couldn't understand was why I kept going back! What did I need from this man, was it because he was my first love? Why did I stay? Why would I keep believing him when the outcome was always the same? Now that I think back on all of this, I know that I was young, immature, insecure, uninformed, and afraid. Who in their right mind would welcome pain? My life was a merry go round or a seesaw and I wanted to get off of it!

I made up my mind that I never wanted to be married again because I felt that no one was serious about a real marriage and men just wanted to play games. I just wanted to focus on being a mother and making a living for my children. I got a job at the Prince Murat Hotel where I met Mr. Leonard Nimoy, "Spock" from Star Trek! I had to throw this in because I was such a Trekkie back then. Ok, I'll quickly tell my embarrassing story:

I worked in food services and had to deliver lunch to one of the rooms. I knocked on the door and a gentleman opened the door and told me to come in and sit the food on the table. Before I got to the table, I noticed Mr. Nimoy sitting on the side of the bed and I yelled SPOCK!; and dropped all the food on the floor. The group of people that were in the room laughed and help me pick everything up, then I ran over to him and asked for his autograph. I told him how much I loved his character and the wisdom that comes from his words, while shaking like a leaf on a tree. He was there because he was a guest speaker for a function at LSU. He gave me his autograph, shook my hand and I went back to the kitchen about to burst because I wanted to tell everyone, but we weren't allowed to.

Now, back to my story….

I moved in with a cousin that lived with her boyfriend in a two-bedroom apartment and another couple in the other bedroom. The other couple would fuss and scream at each other all of the time and they reminded me of what I was running from. He had an on again, off again girlfriend that constantly moved in and out. The living room was my bedroom and I was grateful for the sofa but trying to get some sleep at night was a nightmare in itself because of the arguing. I don't know how my cousin and her boyfriend could sleep through all of this! One night the girlfriend walked out with her suitcase and we never saw her again. The guy's name was Darryl and he offered me the bedroom and said he would take the sofa, but I declined. It was a tempting offer, but I didn't want any trouble and I didn't know when on again, off again might return and I definitely didn't want her to think that I was with her man.

Darryl and I started talking more and having discussions about relationships. He would ask me the "why women" questions and I would ask him the "why men" questions. He was cool and I enjoyed our conversations and debates.

He too was easy on the eyes and handsome. Slightly bow-legged with a small gap in his front teeth that I thought was cute. I tried hard not to stare at him because I had already had enough drama in my life, but he was very handsome and became a wonderful friend. After a few months passed, he asked me out and I said yes. I liked the way I felt around him. He was respectful and attentive to me and I loved being in his presence. I knew it was happening again, I began to like him, and I tried to pretend that I didn't. He always made me laugh, this was refreshing compared to what I was accustomed to. We would go out to lunch, a movie or go grab some food but he was easy breezy, and I loved that about him. I thought, this is what I want. One day he took me to his family's house, he wanted me to meet his mom and brothers. I asked why and he said because he liked me. Well I thought that you bring someone to meet the family when you love them, not like them, but anyway, I went but I made sure they knew that we were just friends. It was so refreshing to know someone so nice and it scared me a little because they all started so nice. We became official and this time, I just expected to have fun. I just expected to have a faithful, non-violent, fun loving boyfriend that would love me and keep me smiling. I wasn't worried about a future, just wanted to capture something I never really had, and that was my teenage years.

Everything was good. By this time, he had moved back to his family home, and I back to mama's but I would spend every weekend with him and his family.

As the months passed, I found out that I was with child again. When the doctor told me how far I was I then realized that I had to be pregnant when I left Rocky. I told Darryl my suspicion and he was a little shaken at first but didn't seem to care because he knew my story. This time I had a beautiful baby girl and I named her Chandra. She looked like a porcelain doll with lots of hair. I was so happy to finally have a little girl! I never thought that at age 21 I would have 3 children, but God blessed me with them, and I was grateful! I told Rocky the truth and I later told my daughter, and she was blessed with two daddies that loved her.

I was at a place in my life where I was at peace and I didn't care what anyone thought about me anymore. I was excited to be a mom and I was thankful for a good man in my life. Darryl asked me to marry him but the thought of that scared me. I just wanted to live together and see how it go first but not marriage! I told him how I felt, and he assured me that my life would be better, so we got married and he enlisted in the army-- another military man! I was happy and at peace and thankful for this man. First husband in the marines, second husband in the army!

After basic training, the kids and I went to Georgia to start our new life with Darryl. We were so excited, but something seemed very familiar to me and it wasn't the military atmosphere, it was Darryl. He was different, almost nervous like, and not so happy. I already knew that boot camp could be hard, but my happy man was gone. I asked if everything was all right and he said yes. We moved into this mobile home and began our life there, but we began to argue. So, I asked the same ole familiar question, "is there someone else?" This time I was going to be out immediately! He said no, but as time passed, he became more distant from me, and I found out that what I thought was another woman was alcohol! Darryl had changed and I saw the same change in him that I saw in Rocky! It was déjà vu! I couldn't believe it! It was a replay of my other life! I remember one night he got so mad at me that he picked me up and threw me into another room, I flew through one room and landed in another! I wondered if the stress of boot camp affected both of these men, because this was an exact replay of before!

I thank God that I wasn't badly hurt but I became scared again, and again he told me that I better not leave him! This time I realized that his lure was alcohol! I found out later that there were women also, but the alcohol was the dominant thing. He started fighting me every time he got drunk but this time, I fought back! I took my children to the bedroom and shut the door and told them not to come out for fear of them being hurt. I knew I couldn't beat him, but I knew how to fight. I had had enough!

I became angry, especially at myself, I couldn't believe that I was going through all of this over and over again. I didn't do anything to deserve this. I didn't do anything but love him. The more I fought, the more I was hurt. That was it for me! I was done! I was definitely out of this. I had to protect me, and I had to protect my children! I couldn't call anyone because we didn't have a phone and on top of that, he put a lock on the outside of the doors so I couldn't leave when he went to work. I couldn't get out of the windows because it had the small panes that you turn with a crank to open and close and nobody could get out of that. I thank God that we never had a fire! He also stopped any communication with my family.

So again, I was stuck with a man that I no longer wanted to be with, and nobody knew what was going on. I endured domestic violence until his time was finished in the military and we drove back to Louisiana. When we came back home, he wouldn't allow me to reach out to my family. They didn't know that I was back home, but I knew that I would have a moment, just one moment where I would be able to contact someone.

We were staying at his father's house who was a very nice man, who was a college professor. One night some of his friends came over and he began to drink. He had one too many and that was my window, after he fell asleep. I knew that was my opportunity to try to get out. I called my daddy, who was a police officer, just like my stepdad, and my dad was very protective and supportive of me. When he found out that I was home and what happened, he was furious! I knew that

I wouldn't have anything to worry about. I told him the whole story and he told me that he got off from work at midnight and that he would be on his way. I knew if anyone could rescue me, it was my daddy.

When my dad arrived, Darryl told him that I wasn't going anywhere. My dad looked at me and said, "I'm going to ask you one question Jean, do you want to leave?" I said yes and he told me to get the children and our things. Darryl came towards me and daddy, in uniform, gun and all, told him "I wouldn't do that if I were you." Darryl's father told him to let us go, that he didn't want any trouble and he stepped back. He said a lot of ugly things, but he wouldn't move as daddy took me and the children out of there, and I never looked back.

I don't know if it was a military thing, but it was the exact same pattern! It started with impatience, then short tempered, then cursing and violence. Between these two men, I had been beaten countless of times, thrown out of the house naked, cheated on, struck with objects, had kerosene poured on me, while threatening to strike a match, locked indoors where I couldn't go out, kicked in the stomach with military boots, black eyes, bloody noses, knocked unconscious, and all kinds of emotional hurts, and why?

I went home to mama and got my own place, shortly after, and the last thing I wanted to see was a man. I just wanted to take care of my children and make a wonderful life for them. I had to obtain welfare to help gain my footing. We struggled so much because it was hard, as a single mom with three kids, but I didn't want my sons to grow up like that, and I didn't want my daughter to think it was ok to be treated like that. At times, we were from pillow to post, living on and off with different relatives, but I got a decent job and bought a car and things started looking up.

Why am I putting all of my business out there like this?

Because I want to help somebody. There are so many women out there, and men also, that are being abused and living in fear for their lives and the lives of their children.

Because I was raised with the motto of what goes on in this house, stays in this house, but what's going on could cost you your life.

Because many women have kept quiet and watched history repeat itself to the point of death.

Because I'm a transparent woman of God, that realizes that we go through things and God brings us out of the fire so that we could help pull someone else out.

Because many women pretend... they live in fine homes, drive fine cars and drink fine wine at the price of a fist, or infidelity, to maintain a lifestyle of security, not realizing that they are in danger, unhappy and empty.

Because I heard my sister and niece murdered while speaking to her on the phone.

I didn't want these kinds of men in my life. I didn't want anything from them. I just wanted a fresh start. I had to live with their secrets most of my life, protecting them while they bust me up and pretending that all was well while living a lie! My children would ask me why I was sad. I always came up with a lie because I didn't want them affected by the poison I drank that turned me into this mean, angry person. I know that I had been wronged by these men and I couldn't let anyone know the hell that was going on in my house. I made a promise to myself that I would never let anyone else ever hurt me again. I didn't want to love anyone; I didn't trust anyone. I became offensive to anyone that tried to get to know me and I just didn't want anyone in my face. I felt that all men were liars, cheaters and dogs, who used women for punching bags!

I try to make choices now by praying first, because I need to know what God knows that I don't know, especially when it comes to who to trust, who to work with, what door to walk through, what job to take or even when or who to walk away from. I felt like something was wrong with me. Why would I keep going through the same thing? I knew I wasn't a bad person, but I couldn't understand these carbon copy men.

As women, we really need to understand how special we are to God. We need to take a long look at ourselves in the mirror and ask God to show us what He sees. When you realize how wonderful and amazing you are, you won't sell yourself short! You won't allow certain things in your life. You won't just stand there and be disrespected, cheated on, lied to or verbally or physically abused.

I didn't know. I was just a young girl trying to figure it out my way and my way wasn't working. I didn't even understand that I was so special to God, flaws and all. I just didn't understand how precious I was to God. It didn't matter what anybody else thought about me, all that matters is what God says about me!

You are the prize in the marriage not the opponent, you are the treasure not the trash and your body is the temple not a punching bag. You are worth waiting for, fighting for and being honored, love, respected, protected and covered spiritually. We have to choose wisely to accept the right partner, not just one to sleep with but someone that you want to wake up to for the rest of your life.

I needed someone that would rescue my heart and help it mend. I needed someone to really see me...

See my pain

See my needs

See my heart

See how discouraged and detached I was

Someone that would love the pain away

Someone to simply see the inner me,

not just my face, body, legs, and
thighs but the core.... inner.....Me.

When I learned who I truly was as a woman,
my mind changed, my expectations changed, and my
actions changed. I began to love myself, and I wanted
someone in my life that would love me the way I now
loved me.

CHAPTER 4

MY KNIGHT CAME AT MIDNIGHT

Midnight - the transitional moment from one day to the next; supposedly the darkest hour of a day.

After going through years of pain from my 2 marriages and even some family hurts, I moved away from everyone. I desired to start my life over again with just me and my children.... my babies, the only constant that was in my life.

We struggled financially but we always had food, we struggled with having our own place to live but we always had a roof over our heads, and I struggled to keep a job because I couldn't afford to pay daycare costs.

We were from pillow to post and I didn't have any outside support other than the system...the welfare system. I didn't know God at that time but I'm grateful that God has always known and provided for me. I would talk to Him, but I hadn't developed a relationship with Him.

I had a childhood friend named Earl. I met him in 6th grade. He came from a godly family.....from a lineage of pastors, his grandfather, and great grandfathers before him. Over the years, he would visit my mom and ask about me and the children. He was very kind and compassionate and easy to talk to, always encouraging and ever ready to help with a solution to any problem. He would tell me about Jesus and the word of God but at that time, I didn't want to hear any of that.

Earl was 6'5, tall and handsome! He was what I envisioned as God's model man, inside and out. He was a well-dressed gentleman, and always smelled good! He had smooth skin and soft, curly hair and the sweetest spirit I had ever witnessed in a man. He was humble but confident, strong and secure. He had earned the nickname, Mr. GQ Smooth in high school, because he wore designer clothes. What I loved about him most was that he was an authentic man that helped me to become a better person. He always looked out for me like a big brother even when he dated other girls. Earl was an awesome friend that I could confide in and feel safe..

He eventually confessed his love for me but I didn't want our friendship to be affected by a relationship, but when I told my mom she said that a true friend would make the best husband because he already knows everything about you and the love and trust was already there.

We started dating, I was dating my buddy! It felt strange at first, but very comforting. I loved the way he treated me and made me feel. I loved everything about this man! It blew my mind the way he treated my children, he truly embraced them as his own and he embraced our relationship with such love and care as to not break me or hurt me as if I were made of glass. He was such a gentleman, opening doors, pulling out chairs, and putting my wants and needs before his own. He always made me feel like it was "Jean's world." I never wanted to be away from him because he made me better and the way he treated my children was amazing!

I watched and waited to see him change but it never happened, he was an authentic work of God. Earl truly was different from any man that I had ever known.

I knew he was an awesome friend, but I never thought that he would surpass that as a mate. He remained kind and humble as I had always known him to be. He wasn't perfect, but he was perfect for me! He was my angel sent from God to rescue me and my children and give us hope again. I thought I was in love before, but I loved this man beyond measure. I know that I love easy and I love hard but what this man did to my heart couldn't compare to anyone else!

We moved in together for about a year or more, because I was still afraid of the marriage thing but after a while he said that he no longer wanted to live in sin that he wanted to marry me, but I just wasn't ready. He was so easy to be with, he did whatever it took to make me happy. He wasn't a control freak or demanding, he was simply kind and gentle, but he took a stand on living in sin.

I remember one day going to the child support office to try to get help and he told me to drop the child support charges because our children had a daddy now. The child support officer told me that all that sounded good but if I dropped the charges and things didn't work out between me and Earl, that I could never get support again and Earl said, that would never happen, that he would take care of us forever and I said ok. We walked out of the office with the lady shaking her head as if to say what a foolish girl!

My children didn't really remember all of the drama that I went through in my earlier marriages because they were younger, and I thank God that they weren't affected by it. I protected them as much as I could, all they really remember is their daddy, Earl. They grew up knowing who their fathers were, but they were raised by Earl and he gave us a wonderful life, yes at times we had our little spats, but they were nothing compared to what I went through in my past.

Earl introduced me to a life that I had never known, the finer things in life like fine dining, designer clothes and shoes, nice cars, motorcycles, boutiques and elegant experiences I had never seen. He would take me and the children out for picnics on the lawn of the state capital and every weekend he did something with the family. We also had our private moments together and I loved how important he made us all feel.

What's really amazing is that he told me in the sixth grade that he was going to marry me someday! I remember telling him "no way church boy, I'm not into that church stuff, that will never happen!"

We got married and had a happy and fulfilling life, shortly after, he led me to Christ! About age 31 we had a son, I named him Earl III, after his father. He is the spitting image of his father, a beautiful baby with curly hair and the same personality as well. At age 35 I had another son that I named Joshua, and he has the build and personality of his father but resembles his great-great-grandfather, another beautiful baby.

He was a wonderful husband and father....so wonderful that one day when I was pregnant, I got angry at him and told him I was leaving. (I wasn't really leaving, just pregnant and grumpy) My children – whom I had before the marriage looked at me and said, "We want to stay with daddy!" I was puzzled, "You'd rather stay with him instead of me?" And they responded, "We love you mama, but we rather stay with daddy."

I knew then that I had made a very wise choice. Earl was truly an awesome man of God. He prayed constantly for me and the children, with me and the children and taught us through bible study nightly. We were faithful at our Church and helped in any way we could to be Jesus in the Earth. When he noticed the children's gifts, he immediately supported them.

My eldest son, Vernon was an amazing artist, his drawings were extraordinarily good, so Earl purchased art supplies for him and enrolled him in art classes. He also encouraged him to step out on his gift and draw for others which included personal portraits as well as all of the art in the high school yearbooks.

My second son, Vance was gifted in music. We had a piano at our house that all of the children played but Earl noticed that Vance was really good. Vance played guitar, saxophone base guitar and keyboard and whatever else interested him, so we purchased all kinds of instruments and traveled with him during his years in the high school jazz band.

My daughter showed us leadership abilities as well as sports. We supported her volleyball, gymnastics and track as well as the pageants and clubs. She was on homecoming court every year until she was queen and whatever she needed all of the gowns and gloves and shoes she needed Earl bought, as well as chaperoned her during homecoming every year.

Earl was great, but I was still damaged goods. I was happy but I was so torn down by my past relationships that I didn't know how to respond to goodness. He was very patient with me, and he took great care of me and the children and raised them as his own and never called them stepchildren, and he never wanted me to work.

God used this man to help heal the pain of my past, He used him to make me feel better about myself. He treated me like I had never been treated before. He loved and protected me and exposed me to a life that I had never known. I finally got to an emotionally healthy place. Life was finally sweet, and I was finally healed, had self-esteem and happy. I asked him why he would marry a twice married woman with so much baggage, he said that he came to restore what he has always loved.

My knight truly did come at midnight. He came during the darkest time of my life, a time when I was just a broken piece of torn down flesh beaten down with emotional pain and mental baggage, and he covered me, and protected me because he came in God's armor and loved me to a healthy place of healing and wholeness. I could finally hold my head up.

I had also lived with the pain of childhood, being called bastard when I didn't even know what that was, because society won't allow you to live that down back then. I had to live with the pain of miscarriages and a stillborn child. I lived with the loss of a best friend to suicide, my sister and my niece being taken away from me in the same day and so much more that you wouldn't believe, but God used this man to bring hope back in my life. He transformed my life, helped heal my hurts and pains, help me trust again and love again and just breathe.

We wanted to help others heal also, so we opened our home for ministry, prayer and bible study. We also ministered to other couples and shared our story. I read somewhere that authentic love can be risky, to love is to be vulnerable and to OPEN your heart, but security lies behind the walls of a CLOSED heart. You either invite the union by opening in love or you secure the isolation by closing down. I thank God for opening my heart again. We were married over 20 years….and then he died.

I don't have words to describe that new pain! Part of me died too. I felt like I was standing alone, sawed in half from my head to my feet….one side of me standing numb, empty, lifeless, void and half dead while the other side of me fell to the ground and eventually died!

What do I do now?

The man that showed me what true love was - was gone; and I wanted to go with him! Nobody had ever loved me this way, ever! Nobody ever treated me so special. What about my children? He raised my three and now he won't be able to raise his own two sons. I didn't want them to hurt like I was hurting. I didn't want their hearts ripped apart like mine. I didn't want them to feel the magnitude of pain that encompassed my soul! We were finally a real family! Not broken any longer; yet still SHATTERED!

My husband was diagnosed with ALS or Lou Gehrig's disease, a disease that affects the motor nerves and restricts movement. He started limping, then went to a cane, walker and finally a wheelchair. For two years, I did everything for him cutting his hair, brushing his teeth, washing his face, bathing him and scratching every itch. He couldn't lie in our bed or the hospital bed that we had in our home because they weren't elevated enough for his comfort so he chose to sleep in a recliner and I slept right next to him on the floor every night so that I could be next to him. I hadn't slept in a bed for months, but I didn't care as long as I was next to him. It didn't matter to me that he couldn't hold me or touch me the way he used to, just being in his presence was all I wanted and needed. I would have lived with him like that for the rest of my life if I had to.

It broke my heart to see my husband going through all he had to endure, but I love him the same and I respected and honored him the same. I didn't mind taking care of him because he took care of me. I didn't mind meeting any of his needs because he met all of mine. But eventually, I needed help, certain things were hard for me to do because he was such a big man.

We had a friend that my husband mentored and ministered to named Michael. We met Mike, as we called him, 3 years earlier when I had a daycare. He was our first client. He had a beautiful baby girl named Marissa and I immediately loved this little angel, but when my husband became ill, I had to close the daycare. I still kept Marissa until I could no longer take care of her and my husband.

Mike would come over to help however he could. He would take Earl to doctors' appointments, bathe him, cook for the family and do whatever he could to help our family as well as give me some much-needed breaks because I still had to take care of our boys. He would also come over just to sit and talk with Earl because he was going through his own rough times and Earl would minister to him and pray with him and encourage him to continue to trust God for His will to be done in his life.

Mike had a financial services business and Earl joined his team before he became ill, he worked part time because he had a full-time job as well. Mike and Earl spent lots of time working together, reading and studying the bible and honestly, I became jealous of the time that was being taken away from me. I guess I was a little selfish when it came to Earl. I understand ministry and I would never interrupt any assignment that God used Earl to fulfill because I knew that Mike was an assignment, and Earl was ministering to him and I wasn't messing with that!

Mike was around so much that he became a family member, a brother to Earl. I remember one day after Earl became ill, he asked me to go to Mike's company meeting because he wasn't getting around as well and he didn't feel comfortable trying to use a walker, so of course I went. During break time, someone I knew from my old church came over to say hello. I hadn't seen her in years, but it was good to see someone else I knew at the meeting. She saw me talking to Mike and wanted to know who he was and was he married. I explained to her that he was a friend of ours and that he was recently divorced. I told her about Earl's illness and that Mike came over daily to help Earl. We continued our small talk, exchanged numbers and she started coming over. Since I knew her reason for coming over was Mike, and I knew that he was 2 years single, I decided to play matchmaker!

I asked Mike to do me a favor and take her out, he really didn't want to because he hadn't dated in 2 years. He wanted direction from God as well for who God had for him, but he said that he would do it for me. They began seeing each other and I was excited because I could get all of time with Earl back!

As time passed, she told me that they were talking marriage, all of this happened so quickly, so my wheels started spinning and I immediately jumped into wedding planning mode! I was excited for Mike because he always told us that he wanted the kind of relationship that me and Earl had, and I got tired of seeing him feeling left out.

One day, while Earl and I was alone, I began to share some of the thoughts I had concerning the wedding, Earl had this very serious look on his face and I asked him what was wrong, he said these words to me:

"Jean, leave this alone, she is not his wife" I asked him who was his wife then and he didn't answer me. He said again, "Leave it alone, you're messing with destiny!"

Somehow, those words shook me to the core. It felt like God himself had spoken those words to me. I left the room without saying a word and I never opened my mouth about it again. Later on, Mike told us that he called it off. He said he prayed and asked God if she was his wife and God showed him that she wasn't.

One day, Earl stopped breathing; he died for a few minutes and came back. When he opened his eyes, he looked at me with tears in his eyes and said he saw a glimpse of glory! He talked about the colors and how vibrant they were and the amazing peace he felt and the presence of God! From that day forward he was never the same, all he would do was look towards heaven, praise and pray. He told me how much he loved me and the children, but he no longer wanted to be here. I cried and didn't want to hear that, but he said that he was only existing here and he wanted to go back to heaven and live. This broke my heart; how could this happen to such a loving man. I didn't want to hear anything about him leaving me, but I knew he was tired; he wanted to be healed or he wanted to go. He would constantly tell me that if you don't have your health, you don't have anything.

This may sound crazy to some of you, but I believed my husband, and he was constantly trying to prepare me, but I wouldn't listen. He told me that he went to the Father on our behalf and promised me that all would be well with me and the children. I cried and didn't want to hear finalities, after all, I was still believing God for his healing. People came to our house daily to visit my husband to pray for him and encourage him, bring food and bless us, but what blessed my soul was the fact that he would pray for them, encourage them, and bless them! Everyone that walked in our door would prophesy the exact same thing, everyone, they all said that God was going to heal him, raise him up and that he would walk again. Everyone! This gave me so much hope, this made me excited and my faith was at a new level and I began to tell everyone that they were about to see a miracle, even the doctors!

EVERYONE. EXCEPT TONI SPEARS!

Toni Spears is a prophet and a wonderful friend. I loved her and her family dearly. They were true people of God and I respected her and her gift. She came over one day and asked me to step outside, I noticed that she was nervous and teary eyed. I asked her what was wrong. She told me that God sent her to give me a message and that she's been struggling with how to tell me. I told her to just say it and she went on to tell me that everyone that has been coming over to see Earl told him that God would heal him, but not on this side of heaven she said. I said what are you saying?! Are you telling me that my husband is going to die?! She calmly said yes. I became angry and said that everyone is speaking the exact same thing and you are the only one coming here with this. I then asked her to get out of my yard. She said God told her that she had to tell me everything. I said "Oh, there's more! Get out of my yard! Please leave!" She continued talking and said that I and the children would be fine because God was preparing a mate for me. I really lost it then! I was in fighting mode and I explained to her that my husband was in the house fighting for his life and you're coming here telling me that he's going to die, and God got another man for me, that's stupid. God doesn't work like that! I told her to get the hell out of my yard! She said wait....I have to tell you who it is! I was so mad, hurt, and shocked! All of the hope and excitement about my husband's healing was shattered! I became so discouraged all over again.

I believed that God was going to heal him because I know He can. Why let him die, who I love and who loves me and send someone I don't love to be my husband.....just heal the man I love.

I, then avoided Toni whenever I saw her and I didn't receive a word of what she spoke! I started to believe again for my husband's healing. The next day I received a call from a mutual friend of Toni and I, named Felicia. She said that she didn't want to be involved in this but that she was just calling to give me a name just in case it was God. I immediately became angry and I knew that Toni had talked to her about this. I said to her, "You're right. You don't want to get involved, don't let Toni cost us our friendship." The next two words from her mouth made my blood boil! She said, "Brother Mike." I said, "What damn brother Mike? Our friend brother Mike? My husband's best friend brother Mike?!" She hung up the phone.

And shortly after - he died.

CHAPTER 5

IN THE CLOSET

" In the closet" has come to mean something that you want to hide; something that you think society is not ready for or won't accept.

That's NOT my case here, after my husband passed, I literally stayed inside of my walk-in closet. I just wanted to run away but I couldn't and the only place of safety and solitude for me was my closet. It was in my master bedroom, and you had to walk through the bathroom to get to it, so it was convenient as well as safe from everything going on outside of it. I felt safe there, and God was there, and I could talk to him and cry on his shoulder there and the outside world wasn't welcomed. It was my safe haven....

I was filled with so much grief, I couldn't function...I couldn't believe that he was gone and left me. I couldn't believe that I was a widow. My two babies were still young, but I couldn't take care of them like they were accustomed to; I couldn't even take care of myself. I slept in the closet at night, whenever I could sleep, and sit in the closet during the day crying and praying to die too. I couldn't eat, I didn't care about hygiene and my hair was already falling out due to the stress of it all. I couldn't cook or clean, I just laid there waiting to die.

This all happened a few weeks before Christmas. We already had our Christmas tree up because I love the holidays and I put everything up on Thanksgiving night, but the tree died also. The branches were hanging down to the floor and most of the ornaments had fallen off. My baby boy Josh had a pet bird and a pet crab, and they all died too. I know that this sounds crazy, but this is absolutely the truth. I took the remaining ornaments off of the tree, picked the rest off the floor and dragged the tree outside as if Christmas had come and gone because more grief had now been added to everything else.

What I didn't tell you was that my grandmother, who I'm named after, died the day before my husband did.

> December 5 my grandmother died
> December 6 my husband died
> December 7 is my birthday
> December 8 the tree, the bird and
> the crab died

After all of these deaths I hurried back to the closet wondering if I was next.

Mike still came over every day to check on us like he'd done when Earl was here. The boys let him in because of course, I was in the closet. He made breakfast for the boys, helped them with their school clothes, and brought them to school or stayed with them until the bus came, every day. He would also pick them up from school and make dinner, to make sure that whatever the boys needs were, that they were met before he left.

I felt like an unfit mother, but I honestly couldn't function as normal. I thought I was having a breakdown. I couldn't think straight, I felt all alone, I didn't have the support I thought I would have and the only person that was there for us was the one that I didn't expect to be there, Mike, after all, Earl was gone so he didn't have to be there.

I had to try to get myself together to take care of the arrangements for my husband's burial. I didn't want to deal with all of this, but I had to. We didn't have a car at that time, but Mike assured me that whatever our family needed, he would be there for all of us.

BLESSING

When we got to the funeral home the director asked for the insurance papers, we no longer had insurance. When my husband became ill and could no longer work, I stopped working to take care of him, and we just didn't have the finances to continue paying for the policy we did have so, that's that. We had a small savings but that was needed to take care of the children and me.

I informed the director of my financial situation and he told me that he would help me, he told me to pick out everything that I wanted and that he would do it all for 3000.00! And that I could pay him in installments. The casket alone was 7000.00. He asked if I had anything for deposit, I only had 100.00 in my purse and I paid that. He informed me that everything would be done as I expected and just pay him as I can. To God be the glory!

He told me to bring a suit back for Earl and other necessities, but I didn't want to go back. Mike said he would do it for me, after Mike gave the director everything, he was about to leave the funeral home when he noticed a woman in a casket that he decided to look at, that woman was my grandmother! I didn't know she was at the same funeral home..

After the services were over, I had enough money to pay at least half of the balance to the funeral home. When I got there, I thanked him for his services and informed him that I was there to make a payment. He informed me that my debt was paid in full! I asked how and he said that people were just coming in bringing money!

To this day, I don't know who they are, but if you're reading this book and you're one of those people, I would like to thank you from the bottom of my heart for your kindness, love and generosity! God bless you!

CHAPTER 6

WHEN IT RAINS, IT POURS

After everything was over, the phone stopped ringing, the house became quiet, people stopped coming over, the months started passing by and I went back to my old familiar place... the closet. I still cried but this time I didn't want to die. My babies needed me and after losing their Da-de as they called him, I couldn't continue to check out emotionally on them. They were all I had left of Earl and I needed them to be that constant reminder of him for me to survive. I needed direction from the Father because I couldn't stay where I was, too many hurtful memories, I had to leave that place, that city and that state. I had to get away from this place of pain, run away from the hurt, reminders and triggers.

I also wanted to get away from ignorance, people that were whispering, gossiping, and spewing lies about me and Mike. It's sad, you would think that a person would see your pain and have compassion but "as a man thinketh in his heart, so is he", an evil man thinks evil things and a righteous man thinks righteous things, and at that time I wondered who was godly and who was working for their father the devil.

It's amazes me how people try to mess up your life with a lie, when their life could be destroyed by the truth, but God told us that we didn't have to fight this battle, just experience the victory and He will shut the lion's mouths!

One of my friends, Suzanne, lived in Dallas where she built a new home and invited me and the boys to live until I got myself established. She is a phenomenal woman and her invitation excited me because I thought that now, I could get a fresh start! My plan was to spend some time with my mom, a month or so, and then move to Dallas, Texas! But that was not God's plan for me, and He never allowed that door to open. I stood still and waited for direction from God because one thing was sure, and that was that God would truly order my steps because this was our lifestyle - TRUSTING GOD!

As time passed, I had gotten so accustomed to sleeping in the closet until I went in to pray, went in to cry and I went in to go to bed! I would lock my bedroom door every night so that Earl III and Josh wouldn't know that their mom was sleeping in the closet. I still had full cry days sometimes to the point where my eyelids would swell so big that my eyes were open, but I could hardly see. I just couldn't adjust to this new life, this life without Earl and the fact that I was a widow at 41.

Mike still came over every day to take care of the boys and check on me, he even managed to get me out of the closet one Sunday to take me and the boys to church where I felt a little comfort until his pastor acknowledged me and announced to the congregation that my husband had died. Why? Why would he say that? I realized at that moment that I wasn't ready! I wasn't ready to be around other people. I thought that being in the house of God would help me, but it didn't that day.

Mike did his regular routine like clockwork, but one particular day after he dropped the boys off at school, he didn't go straight to his office like he usually did, he came back to the house to get me out of the closet. He wanted to take me outside for a walk to get some sunlight and fresh air and just talk. He wanted to make sure that I could take care of the boys on my own and that I would be ok. I interpreted that as he was ready to do his own life now, so I told him that he was a Godsend and that I appreciated everything that he had done for Big Earl, me and the children but that Earl was gone now and that he didn't have to worry about us any longer. I went on to say that I knew that he was ready for a wife and that it was his time to go on with his life...and at that moment, it began to rain. I continued to walk as if the rain wasn't even there after all, I felt the sunshine leave me when Earl left me.

I wasn't ready for what was about to pour out of his lips. "Jean, please don't get upset with me for what I'm about to say because I don't understand it either, but you and the boys ARE my life. You know that I have always loved Earl and the rest of the family but somehow it's like a veil was lifted and I realize that I love you and the kids."

I was speechless, and angry, and confused and honestly, I wanted to slap his face off. But, I didn't, because after all he was the only person that was coming around to help us; so I just stood there.

Then he got down on one knee, in the rain and asked, "Jean, would you give me the honor and the privilege of taking care of Earl's family by marrying me?"

I immediately said, "I don't love you like that! I love Earl and I always will!"

He said, "I believe that you'll grow to love me one day."

I was shocked! I was shocked! I couldn't believe my eyes nor my ears!

At that moment, I was trying to come up with something to say but the shock of it all was so overwhelming. I began to explain that someone out there was probably waiting for him and that he should pursue his quest elsewhere, but it was as if he heard none of that. I told him that we would be ok again and that I would stay with the boys about 3 years before I went back to work, then he said that he would never want me to work, that he would take care of me the way his father took care of his mother and that she never worked a day in her life.

As I walked away the rain started pouring, all kinds of thoughts flooded my mind, raining memories of the past but pouring confusion and controversy in my future. All I could do was think about Earl and my children and wonder what path that God truly have for us. I heard all kinds of voices in my head, the people, the prophets, my family and friends, and I heard Toni Spears, was she right? I had never told one person what the Lord spoke through Toni Spears, I never spoke it out of my mouth because I never received it. What would my children think anyway? I remembered Earl's final words to me.

At the hospital, Earl said that he was grateful to God for the years that he gave us and for all of our children and that he was thankful that I was the mother of his children. He told me to go on with my life and live it to the fullest but don't deny his children a father. The last words from his lips was "I love you Jean" and he drifted away.

CHAPTER 7

I STOOD
IN THE
FLAMES

I had to really get away from it all so my mother, my sister Lorna and I decided to take a road trip to Houston to visit my sister Nedra for the weekend. My first lady, called me with a message from Vikki Johnson, a wonderful woman of God that use to come to Louisiana and minister at our church from Maryland. Vikki was a very cool, straight forward, beautiful person and I admired her charisma especially as a leader. She told my first lady that God wanted me to read a book called "I Stood in the Flames" by Dr. Wanda Davis Turner. I purchased the book and took it on the road trip. I started to read while on the road and I couldn't put it down. It spoke directly to me, it spoke to exactly where I was, and it was giving me direction from the Lord! The entire trip I was embracing that book. There wasn't a lot of interaction with my family because I couldn't put it down! My sister Nedra, asked me why I came on the trip because I wouldn't go shopping or to the restaurants or anything, I stayed at her house and listened to God speak to me through this book.

It was a book about a woman of God that lost her husband after a mission trip and God told her to remarry. I knew that this was the will of God for my life and it was confirmed by countless personal prophecies but to me, it still didn't make sense to me, especially the Mike part, so, I prayed that night and I asked God, if that was really His will for me to tell one of my children.

After returning home from Houston, My son Vance came over and told me that God showed him something that upset him. I asked him what, and he said that God showed him that he was preparing a mate for me and he said he told God that he didn't like that. He said that God told him that he didn't care that this was His will for my life.

Then my son looked at me and asked, "You already know, don't you?" I said yes; then he asked me who. I didn't want to tell him because again, I wanted to make sure that this was God, so I told him to ask God. He came back a few days later and said God showed him "white boy". I didn't respond and so he did, "I can see that."

Mike is Creole, fair skinned and beautiful. He is very handsome with wavy hair. When I first saw him, I thought he was Italian. When he enters a room, all eyes are on him. He's eye candy, fashion model material that will definitely get your attention. He is very kind and caring, BUT the fire was turned up seven times hotter when word got out that Mike asked me to marry him. It was so bad that I thought we would be stoned or tarred and feathered! What truly shocked me was that the people that I thought would be there for me were AWOL and some of the believers were unbelieving.

All of these emotions running out of control and I don't know what to do, because I'm passionate about being in the perfect will of God for my life. God was definitely still talking, and people were still gossiping, haters were hating, our families were confused, and I'm grieving, confused and looking like a deer caught in the headlights!

And here comes a sweet moment......

My 6-year-old baby, Josh, walked up to Mike and said, "Mr. Mike, since da-de is with Jesus in heaven, could you be my daddy now? And Mike said, "I would be happy to be your daddy."

CHAPTER 8

PROPHECIES EVERYWHERE!

Coming out of a store one day, an elderly lady called out to me to get my attention. I thought maybe I'd dropped something, or she needed help. When I walked over to her she said "I don't know if you understand spiritual things but when you passed by me the Lord told me to tell you that it is His will that you marry that man. I broke down right there, I couldn't hold back the tears! She hugged me and said "that's a good thing" but she didn't know my story. She didn't know that I was recently widowed. She didn't know everything surrounding this.

Everywhere I went, I promise you, I ran from prophetic words and prophetic people, but you don't know who the gift rests on. So how can you escape it? I have a friend named Debra whom I hadn't seen or talked to in years. She called, asked how I was doing and then she told me that she was praying, and God told her to ask me how long will I be disobedient to what he has clearly told me to do? This time, I got scared because I never want to blatantly disobey God.

My baby sister said that God put Mike in our lives for such a time as this. That he was grooming him for this.

My pastor and Mike's pastor said the same thing and gave us their full support as well.

Another prophet said the same thing.

Then this…….

My neighbor's husband had a dream, he was a musician that played for churches and weddings etc.

In his dream, he was playing at a wedding, but he didn't know whose wedding it was. When the back doors opened, he saw me, and Earl walking down the aisle and thought that we were renewing our vows but halfway down the aisle Mike walked from the front of the church and met us down the aisle. He wondered what Mike was doing there. When Mike got to us, Earl took my hand and put in Mike's hand and then Earl just disappeared. I cried because God kept speaking and showing me, but I was just stuck. Stuck in my own way thinking that it was too soon. I asked for a sign and he gave me many. My next move had to be one of obedience, but how.....when.....

And yes, Mike and I did ask Toni Spears for forgiveness. She was right! NOW, how do I tell my family? How should I expect my children to feel or understand? I'm told to marry someone I've never dated, someone I was never interested in, someone I only loved as a friend not a love interest, and someone that's going through his own pains. This truly is an arranged marriage, arranged by God for His glory. Now, I'm becoming a widow bride.

We had to tell our families and that didn't go well on either side, no one agreed, no one understood, not even me. We told our friends with only a few supporting us. By the time it really was exposed our name was mud. I don't care how much we tried to explain what God said nobody believed it, not even the believers!

We would be stared at and pointed at and someone even lied that we had an affair while my husband was alive, but I thank God for the people that did stand with us that knew better. At this point, God told us not to explain anymore! He told us not to worry because He was going to shut the lion's mouth!

CHAPTER 9

WEDDING DAY

The day of our wedding, I didn't feel like a bride. I hadn't shopped for a dress or gotten my hair or nails done. I didn't have a makeup artist to do my makeup. I didn't have a bouquet of flowers with the fragrance of love and joy. I felt like I was about to walk back into the church toward my husband's coffin. No one will ever know the conflict of thoughts battling in my mind, the tsunami of emotions and the constant grief that just stayed there. Then I heard the words, "obedience is better than sacrifice."

I got up, did my hair and makeup and threw on a purple church dress and waited for my friend Lina to pick me up. Still a plethora of thoughts invaded my mind. I felt like a failure. How could I do this? God, how could you ask me to do this? Who's going to believe this is you?

When Lina walked in she wore a wonderful silver suit lined with a shiny trim, just beautiful. I told her that she looked like the bride and she asked what I was going to wear, and I said, "this is it". She said "no ma'am, now I understand why the Lord had me put this on because I wasn't going to wear this", and she told me to take that dress off and gave me her suit to put on. She has always been a true friend to me, always wonderful to me, but I didn't expect her to do that for me, but now, at least I look more like a bride.

We had a small intimate wedding at one of Mike's friend's home, Maurice and Alisha, with only a few friends and even fewer family members. We didn't have a lot of support, but God kept encouraging us and told us to just trust him and don't worry. God is so awesome, he even showed us the people in our circle that were talking about us and smiling in our faces, but just like in the Hebrew nation in Egypt in the bible, the more they tried to oppress us, the stronger we grew!

That day was a day like I had never experienced in my life. I was sad, yet excited, couldn't make sense of all of the emotions I felt, especially the emotion of betrayal to Earl and my children but most of all, I felt like I betrayed my own heart; but peace came when I felt the Lord's presence, and my obedience to God.

The ceremony was short and sweet, my sister Lorna and my friend Cyndie stood with me as my maids of honor. Cyndie showed up with flowers, the groom's boutonniere and a lovely bouquet for me that I knew nothing about! Lina purchased our cake, Mike's church provided everything for our reception and honeymoon, Cyndie and her husband Earl, took us to Sullivan's for our first dinner together as a couple and the only thing we paid for was the marriage license. God provided everything, all we had to do was show up.

After the wedding we headed to New Orleans, neither one of us could believe what we had just done! We had a chance to really talk and ask each other things about each other that we didn't know, but I feared what was supposed to be next.

The closer we got to the hotel, the faster my heart began to beat as I questioned myself yet again. Once inside of the room, I immediately went into the bathroom. I was in the bathroom almost 2 hours, I had to pray! Mike kept calling out to me asking if I was all right, but I had to talk to my Father as well as deal with some anxieties. This is Brother Mike; I can't let him see me this way! How can I escape this part? I had so many questions flying around my head, but I knew that I had to eventually come out of that bathroom. The suite had a jacuzzi in the room with the bed and Mike had candles lit all around the jacuzzi, by the time I came out of the bathroom, most of the candles was almost burned out, but he comforted me with just two words…"Let's talk."

Our life started so different than anything I had ever experienced. I had never married a man that I didn't date or was intimate with, but I thank God that I didn't have to live with any guilt. I knew that the one thing I could do was hold my head up knowing that I had never slept with this man until I married him, and that, I will be grateful for, for the rest of my life! It's awesome when you do things God's way, you don't have to live with regret and shame the rest of your life. It doesn't matter what lies people tell, what matters is what GOD knows!

We were two people that were brought together by the love of one man, and I was able to still grieve because he was grieving too. I was still able to be angry because he was angry too. I was able to have my thoughts of the past with Earl because he had his also. We were always able to share our thoughts and times with Earl with each other and how we missed him together. I know you may feel a certain way about what I'm saying, but these are my thoughts, and this is my story and I thank God that He backs me up.

I wondered how we would get closer and it's amazing how all of the opposition brought us closer. All of the ignorance made us cling together because we felt like we were all we had, but the most important factor in all of this was God! He truly blessed us, favored us, and opened impossible doors for us that I would have never imagined!

Now, the real journey begins....

CHAPTER 10

4 SUITCASES AND A TOOLBOX

Wе had a revival at our church and a prophet from Houston, Texas ministered. Mike and my son Vance attended. The man of God called my husband up and said this; "everybody around here is talking about you like a dog, but I'm here to tell you that God said, it is His will!' I thank God that he truly had us covered and we no longer had to defend ourselves, He was working everything out for us.

Sometime later, my daughter, Chandra and I attended a women's conference where a prophetess called her up and told her that the Lord said he would be moving her to the east coast, to New York. I went up and stood behind my daughter to cover her as a woman of God and as her mother. The Prophetess asked if I were her mother and she then said that I too would be on the east coast but in Baltimore, Maryland. I was not trying to hear that because I still wanted to go to Dallas, Texas. I didn't receive any of her words for me, but I received them for my daughter. When she was in high school, she said that after college she was moving to New York. In fact, she wrote that in her senior. memory book so I knew that was God. (She did eventually move to New York!)

One Thursday evening Mike came home from work, a construction job; he told me that the job had ended but they gave him a choice, he could go to Aruba where a job would be waiting for him with awesome pay plus per diem, or he could apply for a job in Baltimore, Maryland. Then the light came on and we remembered the prophesy, and Mike said "we got to go to Baltimore!"

We told our families on Friday and boarded Amtrak on Saturday. That night, while on the train, while my family was asleep, I was awakened. The train was moving extremely fast, so fast that all I could see was a blur, so I began to pray for our safety. As I was praying, I heard the Lord say, "tell him there's going to be a freeze on hiring but go back." I didn't tell him this while on the train. I waited because if I would have said that he would have headed back to Louisiana.

We left Louisiana with 700.00 that's all we had. We paid bus fare from Baton Rouge to New Orleans for 4 people, train fare from New Orleans to Baltimore for 4 people and were supposed to pay for an 80 pound toolbox, but because we were running late and almost missed the train, they just threw the toolbox on the train and told us to hurry and get on. 80 pounds free! By the time we made it to Baltimore, we only had 350.00 left! that's it, no job, no family or friends, no place to stay, but we had faith and we definitely had God and he provided one contact for us and that was a man from Mike's job name Joe that moved to Baltimore to work also. All we had was his phone number and knew that he was at a place called Welcome Inn, we didn't have an address or anything.

When we arrived in Baltimore, we tried to find a hotel to get some much-needed rest and could not find any in the city due to a large conference that was being held that booked out all of the hotels. We went to customer service for help and they too couldn't find not one hotel in the city. They found one in a city called Towson. We got in a cab and headed to Towson.

We finally got to the hotel and began to unpack, while unpacking I heard the Lord say, "stop what you're doing, and step outside and look to your left". Without saying a word to anyone I did what he said. When I did, I screamed with excitement because I saw a sign that said "Welcome Inn" right across the street! I told Mike that Joe was right across the street! Mike didn't believe me, so he called Joe and told him that we were in Maryland and that we were at a hotel in a place called Towson, and Joe crossed the street and came to our hotel! God is so awesome, he strategically placed us directly across the street from the only person we knew in this state! Talking about divine appointment!

Joe told Mike that he could ride to the jobsite with him the next day to apply for a job. when Mike came back to the hotel the next day, he looked sad and said that he had bad news....I said "I know, there's a freeze on hiring", he asked me how did I know that and I told him that God told me while we were on the train and he also told me to tell you to go back. Mike went on to explain to me that they told him that they were not hiring one more person, it's a freeze and I went on to explain that GOD said GO BACK!

The following day, Mike reluctantly went back, just to shut my mouth and the same man he talked to before told him that he explained to him yesterday that they truly were not hiring any longer. As Mike was about to leave the building, another man asked if he could help him. Mike explained the whole story to him about him and his family coming from Louisiana and how he came on yesterday, he knew about the freeze, but his wife told him to come back. The man asked Mike to step into his office and they talked. After a while, the man made two phone calls and shortly after, two men came in his office. The man told the two men "I don't care which one of you hire this man, but I want him hired today." Favor! Mike brought home 1600.00 weekly.

God gave him so much favor on that job until when the job was finished, Mike was the last one to leave and the supervisor he was under brought him with him to his new jobsite.

We lived at the hotel for 3 months because the job site was over an hour away and we had to live close to Joe for a ride because we didn't have a car yet. The time for school to start was upon us and we needed to find an apartment. We found an apartment closer to the job site but our credit was "shot" and the manager denied us, now here comes God....another lady came in that worked there, I don't know what her position was but she looked at us, looked at our application and said "I have a good feeling about these people" and we moved in, but we still didn't have a car and now we were an hour away from Joe.

Mike's supervisor and his family grew very close to us. They even gave me a surprise birthday party for my birthday and babysat the boys sometime to allow Mike and I to go to dinner. We took a trip to Roanoke Virginia once to find property to start a business, but that part was not God's will for us. They truly were our new family!

Mike's supervisor's name was Mr. Pete, and Mr. Pete's wife and daughter took me shopping one day. Mike was with Mr. Pete somewhere and suddenly Mike came into the store and asked me to come outside. When we got outside of the store, Mr. Pete was standing next to a car that I didn't recognize.....yes, he took Mike to buy a car.

Funny thing.....back to the apartment manager. When the job ended, we had to move again because the next jobsite was in Baltimore. The apartment manager begged us to stay. He made all kinds of offers and discounts for us to stay and said that we were model tenants and integral people, the best he ever had! God's hand was on us in everything! The favor of God was and still is unbelievable!

CHAPTER 11

IT'S ALL GOD!

My story is not a fairy tale, and Earl was not perfect, just perfectly used by God for me. It's my reality of someone that God used in a healing process. Earl and I were married over 20 years. It was not all perfect, but it was great, and God alone brought us through every obstacle. I understand now why my first marriages didn't work, it's not just the fact that we were kids, but the primary reason is because God wasn't in it.

My vow was fulfilled to God, Earl was there until "death did us part." In sickness and in health, to love and honor, in good times and bad, broke or comfortable, angry or happy, he was there with one thing on his mind, loving and taking care of what was precious to him, his wife and children. I have so many amazing memories that I will never forget, of a man that rescued me, picked me up and loved me to a safe place, no matter what condition I was in. A man that nurtured my walk in God and taught me how to live and love truthfully and righteously in ways that pleases God, putting God first in all things and trusting God completely! I will forever be grateful to God for sending me this angel to show me what pure love was and leaving me with the most precious part of him, our boys, Earl III and Joshua.

My journey continues, it's ironic that God used Earl to groom Mike to walk in the ways of God and become a better person. Truth be told, many times I wanted out of this marriage to Mike, but God would tell me to stand still. As of today, Mike and I have been married for over 21 years. We went through extreme growing pains, after all, I married someone I didn't know outside of being a friend. I learned who he really was, and it wasn't always pretty, but God showed me the hurt and pain that he too was suffering and the healing he also needed. I couldn't just look at what I was going through but I had to consider that this man was an injured soldier too, but my biggest struggle was that he wasn't Earl and I know that's not fair but its truth. I had to learn a lot of things about me in this marriage and what I needed to change because God told me something that changed my life forever, and that was, "I WANT YOU TO BE TO MIKE, WHAT EARL WAS TO YOU." Selah!

One thing I need you to understand is that God knows what's best for you, He loves you with an everlasting love. There is NOTHING you can do to stop God's love and yes, He hates sin, but He loves you! I tried it my way, I tried doing what made sense to me, it didn't work, and it was not fulfilling.

I didn't plan my life the way it went, but now after living it thus far, I wouldn't change it for anything. I would have never believed that this would be my story. This change in my life made wonderful changes in my children's lives. God opened the doors for all 5 of my children to go to college and a few of them have double degrees. God opened doors for world travel to lots of different countries. Doors for some of them to start their own businesses. I am not boasting about these things, but I am boasting about my God, because he opened these doors and made this all possible.

I'm still in awe when I think about where I came from and where I am now because of a faithful God that I gave my life to and stopped trying to run it myself. I read this on Facebook, and while I don't know who wrote it, it blessed me,

> *"Know the Pilot You relax on a plane even though you don't know the pilot. You relax in a ship, even though you don't know the captain. You relax on a bus, even though you don't know the driver. Why don't you relax in life knowing that God is in control?"*

So, I gave my life to God and he has full control. He knows things that I don't know. He sees things I can't see. He hears conversations that I cannot hear. He loves me, He saved my soul, He's given me all things concerning life and godliness, He sacrificed his only son so that I can have eternal life and that's good enough for me to trust him completely!

You may be thinking that I'm one of those Jesus fanatics, I AM! I have watched God work miracles in my life for a long time now and all praise and honor and thanksgiving goes to him and him alone! If I'm going to be crazy about anyone, I told you, it's Him!

I believe in life, that you do have assignments. I know that I was Earl's assignment and then Mike was mine. I believe that God put certain people in your life for a reason, a season and some are there forever. What that specific assignment is, is up to God, but they're there to help you, guide you, direct you even bless you, but God is the only one that gives your life true purpose.

I would always dream for amazing things for my children's lives, but somehow I didn't think about me, but God thought about me and gave me wonderful experiences in my life. I never thought that I would never work again and be taken care of, I never imagined that I would travel or purchase 2 homes and still have the freedom to be me and live, but it all starts with, believing Him, Trusting Him and being obedient to Him.

You have to know who God is and who you are in Him! Once you get to know Him, you can take your power back!

CHAPTER 12

TAKE YOUR POWER BACK!

I gave away my power and now I'm taking it back! I never knew who I truly was, I allowed people to define me. All I have ever known was how to be a people pleaser, how to try to just fit in, how to please everyone all around me and I hated the way it made ME feel. I felt mechanical and robotic, "do this Jean, do that Jean" but never "Jean how do you feel about this or Jean what do you want." I was raised to walk in obedience even before I knew God, but I became rebellious, disobedient and trying to find my own way and please the inner me, tired of being the robot, the follower, the wife of this man and that man until I lost me! God truly used Earl with my self-esteem he helped me to a place in my life where I had to stop people pleasing, stop obsessing overweight, stop caring what people thought or what they expected of me and find ME.

I had to walk away from people obsessed with trying to control my life, telling me what to do and what not to do while watching them do the exact thing they tried to control me with. I truly thank God for His word that tells me everything that I need to know. I'm not promoting rebellion, but we have to trust the mind that God gave us and allow Holy Spirit to lead and guide us.

I thank God that I'm free, loosed from the shackles of the opinions of man (my next book), especially when I can discern the spirit that's operating through some people. As I think back over my life, I struggled because I didn't believe in myself and I brought all of this craziness into my marriages. How horrible to tear someone else's life up because someone else tore yours up but thank God for people that come to restore and love you enough to stand in the fire with you or pull you out!

I had to learn to make my own decisions as well as mistakes, I had to decide what I will or will not allow. I had to trust my God given instincts and abilities, and I truly had to stop caring what people say.

My mother would always tell me to take a look at the one that's judging you and whatever I'm going through would be a walk in the park compared to some of their stuff. This may sound mean, but she was right. We all have skeletons in our closets, we all have things that we regret or things were not proud of or don't want anyone to know, but if we, with God's help could change ourselves then we could be a blessing to help someone else through their experiences.

I have been in the ashes of defeat, failure, misery and pain....at times I have been the residue burned by life experiences. I have lived in dark and unproductive places in my mind, emotions and even some relationships, but thanks be to God who causes me to triumph! I had to be willing to change my mind and turn from my sin. I had to repent to God and some people. I have always believed that Jesus Christ was the son of God and that He died, was buried and rose from the dead. I invited Jesus into my heart and life as my personal Lord and Savior and I watched my life change from a path of destruction to walking and living in the will of God. Whatever you may be experiencing right now, God is right there. Invite Him in your heart, let Him be your best friend, let Him give your life the purpose that you've been seeking for a long time! To God be the glory!

This is what was executed in my life to help me and strengthen me to continue my journey. People will always judge, gossip, hate and talk about you but the most important thing is what YOU think about you. Like I said earlier, when Mike asked my hand in marriage, we were talked about, but what God said and what we believed was all that mattered. Now 21 years later, I'm still getting breakfast in bed and I have heard the words "I love you" every day since my wedding day, whether we're upset with each other or not, even when I'm too angry to respond to him.

What I learned was that my faith does not rest in the wisdom of men, but in the power of God; and He is awesome enough to correct me when I make a wrong decision and lead me down the path that I should take. So, no matter where you are right now, LOVE YOURSELF! Hold your head up high and show your awesomeness. Be confident in who you are. God made you special and He can use all of you!

Taking your power back also means doing what's best for you and your situations. Through all of the drama I've gone through in my life, I have developed all kinds of health issues, like high blood pressure, acid reflux, multiple surgeries and more. I was told by my doctor that most of the illnesses I have are due to stress. My issue with weight is due to stress and emotional eating, so now I'm doing what I need to do to take my power back in all of these areas. I'm trying to live a healthier lifestyle now being more active and eating healthier. I walk away from stressful situations and I have stopped trying to be Ms. Fixit, for other people's problems.

I have learned what belongs to me and what doesn't, and I wasn't built to carry everybody's mess. God intended for us to have sound minds, but we often allow someone into our lives that causes confusion, and depression and abuse, and all these things affect your mind and your body. Whatever area in your life that you have given your power away, take it back and began to rebuild your life one brick at a time. Some of these bricks are self – esteem, your mental, physical, and emotional health, your surroundings, or relationships, only you know what they are. Love yourself enough to take your power back!

CHAPTER 13

MOVING FORWARD

It was not easy trying to move forward when you're hurting, angry and know that you have been wrongfully judged, but the first step in moving forward is forgiving! Forgive and release the resentment, the wrongs done to you, the way they treated you, just release it all; you will never forget it, but you can't allow it to control you!

I HAD TO FORGIVE MYSELF!

I had to forgive myself, for thinking less of myself.

I had to forgive myself for letting my children down and not taking control of my decisions.

I had to forgive myself for every weak area and every area of abuse I allowed into my life.

I had to forgive myself for being bait for weak relationships that weren't strong enough to stand on their own but had to use me as a crutch.

But I also had to forgive others!

I had to forgive Rocky and Darryl, no matter what happened. I had to be mature enough to accept their apologies and free myself of any anger, hatred or hurt.

I had to forgive Cliff, because he wasn't secure in himself and that was evident in his actions.

I had to forgive the liars and haters because they were empty, unhappy, and needed to use me as fuel to fire up their own lives.

I had to forgive Earl for dying and leaving me.

I had to forgive Mike for every bump along the way.

I had to forgive them all!

But most of all, I had to forgive, because God forgave me, and saved my soul, by the blood of Jesus Christ! He gave me my life back!

It's impossible to free yourself when you're bound. Bound by hatred, unforgiveness, or anything that has control over you. You have to learn to let go, let go of it all. It doesn't matter what has happened you have to want to be free to live, to thrive, to soar! I couldn't hold on to the ashes. I had already been through the fire. Why hold on to the ashes? Cleanse your hands and your heart of the soot. Chip away the cement of anger that has had you stuck in the same situation for years. It's your time! I had to think about what someone else may be going through that would cause them to change, or cause them to hurt you, there's always more to the story. I didn't share every part of what I went through in this book because that's not important, what's important is that ANY kind of abuse is not ok, and if you find yourself in it, you have to make a choice!

All of my former husbands are gone now, they are no longer on this Earth and I chose to remember the good things about them all, because in the midst of all the ugly stuff, good things came out of the ashes…. Some of my children came out of those ashes. I learned so much from each of these relationships that's still a part of my life today. I want to help somebody, because I don't want anyone to go through some of the things

I went through, but you have to know the difference between what's just good times and what is long lasting.

I have to continue to move forward because God has promises for me and my family that have not been manifested yet and I am excited to see what he has in store for us!.

You can't move forward without changing your way of thinking. It's not easy trying to move forward when you're numb, because numbness paralyzes you, puts you in a state of shock! You can't calculate your next move when you're trapped, you have to be free to move because freedom requires movement! Don't let what people say stop you from walking in a healthy place! People will always have something to say, but what they say shouldn't matter to you, I told you, what YOU say and what GOD says is all that matters. Free yourself from "the people" syndrome, the people say this, and the people say that! WHO CARES! Do it for yourself, because you're worth it, do it to have a better life, but most of all be free and learn to soar above all of the negativity that has kept you where you are.

If someone is freed from prison and the gates are opened but they refuse to move, they will never experience the new chapter of their life that's right there in front of them on the other side!

If you open the door of a birdcage, but the bird refuse to exit, he will never know what it feels like to fly again and soar!

If you're caught in a fire, and not try to fight your way out, you will be burned and that's what I did, I allowed myself to be burned over and over and over and it didn't stop until I made a move.

Moving forward also mean not constantly going backwards. You can't go forward and backwards at the same time. You have to accept reality and make your decision based on what's best for not only you but your children. YOU HAVE TO ACCEPT TRUTH! That doesn't mean that you have to stay in a bad relationship. I had to accept the fact that one of those men just wanted a good time. It is what it is! Don't look at your situation through rose colored glasses but see clearly, the situation you're in and embrace your truth.

So many times, I said, "I love him and he's really not that bad." Yet, I was the one, standing there bleeding. I would say, "maybe if I change, he might not." While looking at myself in the mirror with a black eye. I would say, "if you do this to me one more time..." and it turned into hundreds of times. I would also say, "but I have nowhere else to go" while picking myself up off of the floor.

When is your enough, truly enough?

This reminds me of a movie I saw with Jennifer Lopez, called "Enough". I cried so much because I saw a lot of myself in this movie. She met a man that was perfect, so she thought, and after she married him and had his child, he began to beat her and disrespect her, and this love of her life turned out to be pure evil! She ended up having to literally fight for her life, but first she had to come up with a plan, she weighed all her options, did physical training and executed her well thought out plan. It's sad the things that some of us have to endure when we only wanted love.

It's real, don't talk or think yourself into fantasy land, open your eyes and see it for what it is! And that's straight up truth because there are some amazing men out there that would be excellent husbands to truly love you. Don't settle for the counterfeit, wait for the authentic. All men are NOT dogs and only one man is perfect, and that's THE MAN - JESUS CHRIST!

CHAPTER 14

TRUSTING GOD WITH MY HURT AGAIN

I know that I wouldn't have survived a lot of what I went through if I didn't come to know God. It's just that simple. When I allowed Jesus into my life, everything changed! My way of thinking changed from always having a victim mentality to become a warrior rising up! My expectations changed and were met. My life became everything opposite of the life I had before. My confidence grew and I felt like a new woman with a head to toe makeover from the inside out!

I had to walk into this marriage hurt, due to my former husband's death, but everything that happened before that was used for ministry because whatever God heals, doesn't affect you anymore. You share it, learn from it, grow from it and gain wisdom from it. I stepped out on faith in God, this time and not man. I know that I need a power, that's stronger than I am, that would order my steps, take care of me and keep me safe from harm, and that's not found in a man, that is only found in God. It was scary when I remarried because I was afraid of going through the same thing I went through in the first two marriages, but I was also afraid of not being treated the way Earl treated me, and my biggest fear was that this husband might die on me also.

I had to trust God, that's all I had, and because I tried it and I knew it worked, I stood on his word and decided to believe in His promises and take that leap of faith. Again, the stresses of the things I endured caused multiple health issues but I'm thankful to still be alive, because many times I thought it was the end… and nobody should have to live in constant fear like this.

I lost my sister and niece to domestic violence and that hurt never goes away. I lost a best friend to suicide, I lost my husband to a fatal disease, a stillborn child and two miscarriages but these traumas opened me to a higher level of love! It made me understand that no one is here forever and that I had to live my best life LOVING!

It taught me these three things:

1. The sacrifice of love - giving of yourself for the sake of someone else, and giving your all, not playing games or playing around with someone's heart.

2. The selflessness of love - concern more with the needs and wishes of others than your own needs, not being selfish but knowing how to love outside of sex or material gain but loving and taking care of someone in times of need.

3. The silence of love – when you don't have to open your mouth, but open your heart, and allow your actions to speak. Doing the right thing, the thing that comforts and secures the heart of another.

Tomorrow is truly not promised to anyone, so I decided to live my life to the fullest.

> I decided to love,
> I decided to forgive,
> I decided to trust,
> And I decided to live.

We don't know what the future holds, we have to accept each day and what it brings, but no one is worth having you in their life, if they can't respect you and treat you like the treasure you are and that's relationship or friendship! But I had a true friend!

It's always good to have someone you can trust; someone you can confide in and trust their opinions. Someone who has your best interests at heart, that person for me has always been my baby sister, Lorna, who we called Baba. She was the baby of three sisters and Nedra is the middle sister. No matter what I have gone through, she has been there for me. We talked every single day, sometimes four or five times a day. I could share anything with her no matter how personal. She helped me in some of my marriages through prayer and wisdom. She was not only my sister but my prayer partner and best friend. We would like to think that we have true friends and sometimes we do, but my sister proved to be an outstanding, trustworthy friend.......I was the last voice that she heard before she was taken from me. I miss you Baba and Kisha and I will always love you. Thank you, Lord, for such an awesome treasure.

CHAPTER 15

LESSONS

It's easy to say, this is what you should do, or this is what you should not do but it's not that simple. Every situation is different and has to be handled differently. I have learned so many lessons from the things I have suffered. The main thing that has come out of all of this is for me is not rushing into a relationship, even if it's just a friendship, take your time and get to really know someone because lots of people come into your life just to get what they want. Some people come in disguised as a sheep when in fact they are wolves. You have to be discerning. I come from a small town in Louisiana where we all knew each other and that made life easier because we knew each other either socially or by reputation.

Now, there are people that sit around all day and plan schemes and ways that they can take advantage of someone. You really have to keep your eyes wide open because the signs are ALWAYS there! I saw some of the signs, but I wanted love! I also learned not to allow anyone to steal my identity, and what I mean by that is not allow a person to change who you are! In my marriages I was 4 different women! I played 4 different roles to satisfy each husband. I had to be the silent type when I'm not a quiet person. I had to be like a disobedient child, afraid to say certain things for fear of being punished, when I was a mother of my own children. I was a rebel turned Christian in another marriage and that was the best thing that happened to me because the real Jean emerged and was able to be herself and live, and I am still that Jean!

I allowed not only husbands to change me, but I had friends and family members try to change me or control my life. I had to learn that God gave ME this life and HE made me who I am, and nobody is going to change that! Being who God has made you is wonderful, and you don't have to chase anyone down for the sake of being loved. When I began to embrace the authentic me, doors opened for me that I never thought I would walk through; great doors that the silent me couldn't walk through.

I learned that no matter who you are, we have all been given the same chances in life and no one is better than you are. God created all men equal, but you have to see yourself in a better way and trust God for the changes you seek.

We all can rise from the ashes, clean ourselves off and start walking that new path in life. We deserve to love and be loved. I believe that sometimes going through the fire makes you a better person, that's what it did for me. It gave me a heart of compassion for not just women but men also that has had their own fires to walk through. It gave me hope to spread to others that this too shall pass, but it also gave me a heart of caution to warn others that this could be fatal. I don't have all of the answers, I'm just a woman that went through the fire and by the grace of God, lived to tell it, but I know that we don't have to live in the fire.

Build your self-esteem to a healthy place. Expect better and become a better person. We can all be better. We all know our areas that need changing....do it for you! Walk in the confidence of who you know you are. Think highly of yourself and love yourself more. You deserve the best and that's YOU!

CHAPTER 16

YOUR
ASHES

Ashes: remains or ruins after something has been burned, proof that you've been through the fire, ashes show all of the dirt you had to endure but it also shows that the fire is OVER!

Even though there's residue, you're alive, you are still here, and the fact that you are, means that there is a chance for a miracle! What you don't realize is that YOU ARE THE MIRACLE! You are a miracle for someone, for something, and you are the answer to a question being asked! You survive all of that to bring you into the new, new life, new lifestyle, new relationship, new city, new job or business, whatever your new maybe. We never go through things without something working for your good and bringing you into the new! Don't look back, look ahead with an expectation of God moving in your situation.

You will still love, you will be loved, God has a purpose and a plan for your life, and it's always for your good. There is someone out there that's looking for a good woman to make his wife. Hold your head up high but hold your hopes and dreams up higher. He wants to prosper you and give you good success, not just success but good success. Trust God in the process, in all of it, and trust Him in the ashes, because something good is coming out of the ashes.

This chapter contains scriptures to help you along the way, as well as questions to help you reflect on your journey:

Psalms 32:8-10 (NIV BIBLE)

> 8 I will instruct you and teach you
> in the way you should go.
>> I will counsel you with my loving
>> eye on you.
> 9 do not be like the horse or the
> mule, which have no understanding
>> But must be controlled by bit
>> and bridle or they will not come
>> to you
> 10. many are the woes of the wicked,
> but the Lord's unfailing love
>> Surrounds the one who trusts in
>> him.

Proverbs 24:19-20 NIV

> 19 Do not fret because of evildoers
>> Or be envious of the wicked.
> 20 for the evildoer has no future
> hope,
>> And the lamp of the wicked
>> Will be snuffed out.

Proverbs 25:19. NIV

> 19 like a broken tooth or a lame foot
>> Is reliance on the unfaithful in a
>> time of trouble.

Psalms 41:1-2 NIV

1 Blessed are those who have regard for the weak.

the Lord delivers them in times of trouble.

2 the Lord protects and preserves them-

They are counted among the blessed in the land-

He does not give them over to the desires of their foes.

Psalms 30:4-5 NIV

4 Sing the praises of the Lord, You his faithful people; Praise his holy name.

5 for his anger lasts only a moment But his favor lasts a lifetime; Weeping may stay for the night, But rejoicing comes in the morning.

Proverbs 2:12-15 NIV

12 Wisdom will save you from the ways of wicked men,

from men whose words are perverse.

13 Who have left the straight paths to walk in dark ways,

14 who delight in doing wrong and rejoice in the perverseness of evil,
15 whose paths are crooked and who are devious in their ways.

Proverbs. 23:7

7 As a man thinks in his heart, so is he

Psalms 118:17

17 I will not die, but I will live and proclaim what the lord has done.

Proverbs 3:5

5 Trust in the Lord with all your heart, and lean not on your own understanding, in all your ways submit to him and he will make your paths straight.

Psalms 27:13-14

13 I remain confident of this: I will see the goodness of the Lord in the land of the living.
14 wait for the Lord, be strong and take heart and wait for the Lord.

Isaiah 54:17

> 17 No weapon forged against you
> will prevail, and you will refute
> every tongue that accuses you. This
> is the heritage of the servants of the
> Lord, and this is their vindication
> from me, declares the Lord.

Isaiah 40:31

> 31 but those who hope in the Lord
> will renew their strength. They will
> soar on wings like eagles; they will
> run and not grow weary, they will
> walk and not faint.

There was a battle going on inside of me, that I had to win!

I had to decide if I was going to stay in the war or win the war, that was my only option, and sometimes your sweet victory is simply….. walking away!

I STOOD IN THE FLAMES - NOW,
I'M RISING FROM THE ASHE!
GOD WILL GIVE YOU BEAUTY FOR ASHES!
TO GOD BE THE GLORY!

CHAPTER 17

REFLECTIONS

QUESTIONS:

How do you feel right now?

_____
_____
_____
_____
_____

Are you happy?

_____
_____
_____
_____
_____

Do you live in fear?

_____
_____
_____
_____
_____

Do you feel safe?

_____
_____
_____
_____
_____

If you could change anything about your situation, right now, what would it be?

_____
_____
_____
_____
_____

How do you feel about yourself?

_____
_____
_____
_____

Fill in the blank: I wish I could

_____
_____
_____
_____
_____

Are you in a place in your life that you dreamed of?

_____
_____
_____
_____
_____

SELF REFLECTION:

_____

_____

_____

_____

_____

_____

_____

_____

_____

_____

_____

_____

_____

_____

_____

_____

_____

_____

_____

_____

_____

_____

_____

_____

_____

_____

_____

_____

_____

ABOUT THE AUTHOR

E. Jean Johnson is a follower of Christ and has been committed to Kingdom work since 1984.

Jean has been married to her husband Michael for 21 years and both are ordained Elders. She is the mother of five, grandmother of 16 and great-grandmother of four. Jean has a heart for hurting women and has led ministries under the leadership of Pastors Joe and Katheran Mitchell, of Greater Faith Outreach Ministries, of Denham Springs, Louisiana. She started a women's ministry called "Help Meet" while living in Baton Rouge, to minister to women of all denominations and ethnicities, as well as guide them to areas of need during times of help. Upon moving to Baltimore, Maryland, she was one of the leaders of Women Walking in Wholeness Women's Ministry, under the leadership of Bishop Ralph and Deborah Dennis, of Kingdom Worship Center of Towson, Maryland. Jean's heart's desire is to simply walk in the purpose that God has predestined for her life, and to encourage women to rise to their God-given destiny!

Pecan Tree Publishing

www.pecantreebooks.com

New Voices | New Styles | New Vision –
Creating a New Legacy of Dynamic
Authors and Titles Hollywood, FL

Rising from the Ashes
E. Jean Johnson

Copyright © 2020 by Emma Jean Rozier
Published by Pecan Tree Publishing

Unless otherwise noted, all Scripture quotations are from NIV are taken from the HOLY BIBLE, NEW INTERNATIONAL VERSION ®. Copyright © 1973, 1978, 1984 by International Bible Society. Used by permission of Zondervan Publishing House. All rights reserved.

ISBN: 978-1-7341058-9-6 - Paperback
ISBN: 978-1-7358295-0-0 - E-book

Library of Congress Catalog Number: 2020918435

Cover and Interior Design by: Charlyn Samson